ADRIANA LUNA CARLOS
Editor-In-Chief, Designer
and Co-Founder

HANNA OLIVAS
Managing Editor
& Co-Founder

NICOLE CURTIS
Director of the SRS
Magazine Division

SUCCESS
SAVVY

SHE RISES
S T U D I O S

**ADVERTISING
OPPORTUNITIES**
Info@SheRisesStudios.com

CONTACT US
SheRisesStudios@gmail.com
www.SheRisesStudios.com

SUCCESS SAVVY MAGAZINE
AUGUST 2024

www.SheRisesStudios.com

LETTER FROM THE EDITORS

Dear Readers,

Welcome to the August 2024 edition of Success Savvy Magazine! We are thrilled to feature Marissa Warren, a globally renowned clinical hypnotherapist and transformational consultant, on our cover. Marissa's journey from personal loss to global influence showcases the power of resilience and healing. Her unique blend of Rapid Transformational Therapy (RTT), Quantum Healing Hypnosis Technique (QHHT), somatic and tantric embodiment, breathwork, and sound healing has transformed countless lives, and we believe her story will inspire you to unlock your own potential.

Success Savvy Magazine celebrates everyday heroes – the entrepreneurs, leaders, and innovators who are making waves in their fields. This month, we bring you stories of individuals who have turned their passions into successful ventures, proving that success isn't just about climbing the corporate ladder but finding joy and fulfillment in every step of the journey. Our pages are packed with actionable insights and resources tailored for all stages of your professional life.

In addition to our cover story, we dive into the latest business trends, explore innovative strategies, and offer practical advice from industry experts. We understand that true success is multifaceted, so we've included thought-provoking articles on work-life balance, mental health, and personal development to support your holistic growth.

As you read through this edition, let Marissa Warren's transformative journey and the stories of other featured individuals serve as a beacon of possibility. We hope you feel the same excitement and inspiration that we did while putting it together. Remember, success is not just about the destination but the meaningful moments and growth you experience along the way.

Thank you for being a part of the Success Savvy community. We are committed to supporting you in your quest for success, fulfillment, and joy. Stay savvy, stay inspired, and keep striving for greatness.

Warm regards,

Adriana Luna Carlos and Hanna Olivas
Editors of Success Savvy Magazine

FENIX TV

PREMIER GIFTING LOUNGE IS HEADED TO

EMMYS WEEK

September 9th - 16th, 2024

SHE RISES
STUDIOS

www.FENIXTV.app
www.facebook.com/fenixtvapp

www.Instagram.com/fenixtv_app/
www.Linkedin.com/company/fenixtvapp

www.sherisesstudios.com
www.facebook.com/sherisesstudios

www.instagram.com/sherisesstudios_llc
www.linkedin.com/company/she-rises-studios/mycompany

TRANSFORMATIVE HEALING: MARISSA WARREN'S JOURNEY FROM GRIEF TO GLOBAL IMPACT

Marissa Warren

Marissa Warren's journey to becoming a globally renowned clinical hypnotherapist and transformational consultant is a testament to her resilience and dedication to helping others achieve profound transformations. Her expertise in RTT – Rapid Transformational Therapy, QHHT – Quantum Healing Hypnosis Technique, somatic and tantric embodiment, breathwork, and sound healing, has made her a sought-after figure in the field of holistic healing. Marissa's approach is deeply rooted in her personal experiences and her commitment to guiding others toward reclaiming their inner freedom and aligning with their soul's purpose.

A pivotal moment in Marissa's life that led her to pursue this path was the loss of her father. This event was a catalyst for her, igniting a "NO MORE" moment where she decided to change the trajectory of her life. Marissa felt a deep calling for more, sensing that she was destined for something greater. She described feeling lost, directionless, and frustrated during this period. However, it was through the grieving process and her healing journey that she discovered the transformative power of RTT – Rapid Transformational Therapy. The results she experienced were nothing short of phenomenal, marking the beginning of her career change and the discovery of her soul's purpose and passion. Marissa's life has never been the same since, and she now finds immense joy in witnessing her clients' transformations and results.

Rapid Transformational Therapy (RTT) and Quantum Healing Hypnosis Technique (QHHT) are two of the primary modalities Marissa uses in her practice. RTT combines elements of NLP (neurolinguistic programming), CBT (cognitive behavioural therapy), psychotherapy, and hypnotherapy. This modality is designed to get directly to the root cause of an issue, remove it from the mind and body, and rewire the subconscious to align with the life the client desires. During RTT sessions, clients are in a state of hypnosis but remain aware enough to dialogue and talk, feeling relaxed and meditative while recalling and addressing past experiences.

On the other hand, QHHT involves past life regression, offering clients insights into their life purpose, past lives, spiritual questions, recurring patterns, and behaviours, as well as guidance on physical, emotional, and spiritual issues. Each QHHT session is unique and varied, with clients experiencing deep states of hypnosis and vivid recollections of past lives. Marissa's decision on which modality to use is based on a thorough discovery call and intake session, allowing her to design a custom treatment plan tailored to each client's specific needs and desired outcomes.

Marissa has numerous success stories from her practice, but one that stands out is a fertility client who had been struggling with conception. After just two sessions with Marissa, this client was able to conceive and eventually held her beautiful baby girl, a moment that Marissa describes as one of the most rewarding of her career. This is just one example of how Marissa's unique blend of modalities can lead to life-changing transformations.

Somatic and tantric embodiment practices are integral to Marissa's approach, focusing on restoring the mind-body connection, maintaining emotional equilibrium, resetting the nervous system, and releasing trauma. Early in her career, Marissa realized that while she could achieve remarkable results in the mind, a disconnect in the body could still cause clients to suffer from dysregulation. The mind controls thoughts, and thoughts control the body; therefore, reprogramming the mind is more effective when the body is in a state of harmony and regulation. Somatic and tantric embodiment allow trauma to be released from the body gently, providing lasting health and life benefits.

Breathwork is another essential component of Marissa's therapeutic approach. It is a simple, accessible, and powerful technique for regulating the nervous system and reducing anxiety. Marissa incorporates breathwork into all her client sessions and practices it herself daily. She emphasizes that during times of stress or anxiety, shallow breathing exacerbates the issue, whereas controlled breathwork can quickly alter the body's physiological response and restore calm. By adjusting the biochemistry within the body, breathwork harmonizes bodily functions, helping individuals to move from a state of survival to one of thriving.

Sound healing, though less common, is a fascinating modality that Marissa integrates into her sessions. Using vibrations and frequencies, sound healing induces deep relaxation and resets the mind and body. Scientific studies have shown that specific sounds and frequencies can alter brain waves, moving the mind into states similar to those achieved through hypnosis. Marissa uses solfeggio and binaural beats during transformation recordings and employs various instruments in one-on-one sessions, sound baths, and breathwork events, enhancing the overall healing experience.

Marissa often encounters clients with internal limitations and negative patterns such as low self-confidence, abandonment wounds, relationship issues, self-sabotaging behaviours, and feelings of being lost or directionless. To help them break free from these barriers, she creates personalized treatment plans that combine hypnosis and somatic embodiment, working on the psychospiritual level to get to the root cause and rewire the subconscious mind. Marissa's goal is to help her clients become unstuck and make lasting changes that align with their desired lives.

Maintaining her own alignment with her soul's purpose and authenticity is crucial for Marissa as she helps others on their transformational journeys. She embodies the practices and tools she uses with her clients in her daily routines, believing that she can only guide her clients as deeply as she has journeyed herself. By continually evolving her own work and maintaining a healthy, intentional lifestyle, Marissa ensures she remains in alignment and can offer the best possible guidance to her clients.

For individuals feeling stuck and unable to make significant life changes, Marissa recommends starting with clarity on the area they want to change and how they envision their life. She emphasizes the importance of incremental, habitual changes and mindfulness in daily activities. By staying persistent and connecting with others on a deeper level, individuals can gradually move toward their dream life.

As an international speaker and author, Marissa conveys the importance of holistic healing and transformational practices by sharing her passion and knowledge. She tailors her content to the audience and event theme, always focusing on actionable takeaways that can be easily implemented. Marissa's ability to tap deeply into people's subconscious and help them break free from limitations is evident in her engaging and inspiring presentations, empowering others to take control of their lives and unlock their infinite potential.

ABOUT HER

Marissa Warren is a globally renowned clinical hypnotherapist and transformational consultant working with RTT – Rapid Transformational Therapy, QHHT – Quantum Healing Hypnosis Technique, Somatic and Tantric embodiment, breathwork and sound healing. I am an international speaker and author.

Marissa embodies these modalities in her life and has used these to heal trauma, make major changes, create transformations and align to her soul's and life's purpose.

For those ready to reclaim inner freedom, break free from past limitations, step into their best life, take action, are ready to uplevel and elevate their life, want to achieve true transformations, and realign with their souls' purpose and align to their own unique authenticity and sovereignty – Marissa is the transformational consultant to help.

Leaving you feeling empowered, living from infinite inner power and potential and stepping into the life and level of success you desire, Marissa will help you tap into your inner magic and utilize your inner resources to step up and shine.

Marissa has a phenomenal ability to tap deeply into people's subconscious to help them break free from internal limitations, negative patterns and behaviors and allow them to move into living their dream life and soul's purpose.

CONNECT WITH HER

- www.marissawarren.com
- www.instagram.com/marissawarren_
- www.youtube.com/@MarissaWarren_
- www.tiktok.com/@marissawarren
- www.facebook.com/marissa.warren.transformational
- www.linkedin.com/in/marissawarren-hypnotherapist-transformationalconsultant

FENIX TV: THE MAGIC BEHIND OUR LUXURY GIFTING SUITE FOR EMMYS WEEK

By Hanna Olivas

As the Chief Branding Officer of FENIX TV, I'm thrilled to share a glimpse of what we're preparing for this year's Emmys Week. There's a certain buzz in the air as the industry's most talented creators, storytellers, and visionaries gear up for one of the most exciting events in television: the Emmys. This year, we're elevating the celebration with our luxury gifting suite, where art, creativity, and the beauty of collaboration come together in one exclusive space.

Imagine walking the red carpet, surrounded by the energy and glamour of Hollywood's brightest stars. Our gifting suite is where the industry's top talent will gather—not just for the luxurious gifts, but to connect, celebrate, and reflect on what it takes to create television that moves, entertains, and challenges audiences. It's a rare opportunity for those who live and breathe creativity to come together and recognize the incredible artistry behind the scenes.

What I find truly inspiring about this event is that it's not just about the glitz and glamour. Yes, there will be stunning red carpet moments, but our focus is on celebrating the magic behind the camera—the untold stories of the creative process. There's something profoundly fascinating about understanding what it takes to bring a show or film to life. Most people see the finished product, but the real magic happens in the countless hours of writing, designing, editing, and collaborating to create something exceptional.

At FENIX TV, we want to shine a spotlight on the unsung heroes—the screenwriters who pour their hearts into scripts, the directors who bring stories to life, the set designers who transform ideas into immersive worlds, and the sound engineers who make every note resonate. The Emmy nominees we honor this year represent the best of this craft. They're not just talented individuals; they're visionaries who have pushed the boundaries of what television can be. Their work challenges conventions, tells bold stories, and leaves an indelible mark on the industry.

One of the things I'm most excited about is offering a behind-the-scenes look at what really goes into making a show or film. We're opening a window into the creative process, revealing the dedication, collaboration, and artistry that many people never get to see. The Television Academy and the Emmys are more than just a night of awards—they're a celebration of the countless hours of work, the late nights, the breakthroughs, and the passion that drive this industry.

Our luxury gifting suite is designed to be a place where art, luxury, and inspiration converge. We've curated a collection of premium gifts from brands that align with our vision of creativity and excellence. But more than that, we want this space to be one where those who've dedicated their lives to storytelling can take a moment to reflect, recharge, and connect with like-minded creators.

As I look forward to this event, I can't help but feel a deep sense of excitement and pride. The Emmy's Week gifting suite is more than just an event; it's a celebration of the craft that I hold close to my heart. It's about honoring the brilliance that happens behind the scenes, the unsung work that leads to those shining moments on stage.

This year's Emmys aren't just a recognition of talent; they're a tribute to the power of storytelling, the creativity that drives our industry, and the extraordinary individuals who make it all possible. We can't wait to celebrate with you and share this incredible experience. After all, it's moments like these that remind us why we fell in love with television and film in the first place—because of the stories that move us, the art that inspires us, and the people who make it all come alive.

CHRISTINE PHIPPS DAVIS

UNLOCK YOUR PATH TO SUCCESS WITH ANOINTED ASSISTANT

UNLOCK YOUR POTENTIAL: ARE YOU READY TO ELEVATE YOUR BUSINESS TO NEW HEIGHTS?

Discover the power of hiring a Anointed Assistant to streamline your administrative tasks, enhance your social media presence, and create compelling content. With Anointed Assistant, you gain access to expert insights and practical tips that drive success. ansform Your Business: Join the ranks of successful entrepreneurs who have harnessed the expertise of Anointed Assistant. Our personalized approach ensures that your unique business needs are met, allowing you to focus on what you do best.

WHY CHOOSE ANOINTED ASSISTANT?

- Administrative Excellence: Efficiently manage your day-to-day operations with our professional administrative support.
- Social Media Mastery: Boost your online presence and engage with your audience through strategic social media management.
- Content Creation: Captivate your audience with high-quality, engaging content tailored to your brand.

Christine@AnointedAssistant.com | www.AnointedAssistant.com

SHE RISES STUDIOS

FENIX TV

EMPOWER**HER** CONTENT DAY

at

Elevate Your Brand Through Creative And Impactful Content!

EmpowerHer Content Day equips attendees with the tools and knowledge needed to craft compelling content for social media, podcasts, and videos.

FEBRUARY 22, 2025

TOTAL ACCESS TICKET: $127

WWW.SHERISESSTUDIOS.COM

HARD WORK + CONSISTENCY = WINS

An Emmy Award nomination, recognition of outstanding achievement in television. For someone who does well just to keep track of remote controls, turn the television on to find the college football game I've been looking forward to, the [insert TV channel or streaming service] movie or series that's said will not disappoint, and the other millions of options of just about anything you want to consume, this event shows me just how much goes into these shows that we get to enjoy. Literal blood, sweat and tears go into your craft for years. You've worked hard, you've earned it. This is your night to shine!

There's no doubt that this evening will inspire some of our youth to follow a path in television. Those already working in television will be encouraged to excel in the fields recognized at this year's ceremony. Partners, spouses, parents, children, family and friends will be proud of this moment for the nominees and winners.

Have you ever noticed there's not an awards ceremony to celebrate an individual's excellence in health? Sure, doctors, hospitals, clinics, and organizations have them but what about us? The ones out here trying to decipher the tons of information now available twenty-four hours a day, seven days a week. The ones looking for, finding, and using that information to find solutions and even beat disease.

What would that award be called? What would be the criteria to be nominated? What would the categories be? What would the trophy look like? For sure we would need to consider, who would host this grand event? Denise Austin gets my vote. Would the public look up to these achievers and try to be more like them? Would having this event change the health score of our world? What does "winning" at health look like? Let me give you a glimpse of what it looks like to me.

The first win came when my A1C returned to the normal range. The second was my cholesterol and blood pressure getting back to normal. The third win was having lab results consistently shift into the positive categories and hardly ever show something of concern on them. The current win is maintaining all of these wins.

You may be wondering so I'll just tell you, yes, there was a significant amount of weight loss that came with these wins. Yes, it was nice to be smaller, look good, even get my confidence and sexy back. Yes, these are wins too. But I couldn't rely on just the scale for my wins. My health had to come first, and the pounds took care of themselves.

What did it take to do this? Just like the many hours, blood, sweat and tears that you put into being your best, I put those into getting my health back to its best. I changed my mindset. I saw who I wanted to become and allowed myself to take that journey. I became obsessed with nutrition. Not dieting, but real food and food that I enjoy. I found a way to get moving again. I committed to myself and stayed consistent. I learned that my health is my wealth.

This is why I will spend the rest of my life helping other ladies do the same. If you, or someone you know, is struggling with weight loss or would like to lower your blood sugar and A1C, I'd love to connect.

Get in touch:

www.ponytailgrit.com
Book: https://www.amazon.com/dp/1960136739
www.facebook.com/groups/ponytailgrit
www.facebook.com/jeanna.h.richards
www.instagram.com/jea3296

Here's to your health and many years of success!
Jeanna Crawford, Certified Nutrition Coach
Ponytail Grit

An Immigrant Nightmare Turned into the American Dream

Personal Journey

Background: I'm Arianny Mercedes, an immigrant from the Dominican Republic. My early life was marked by significant challenges, including fleeing gun violence and systemic inequalities in my home country with my family. Despite these hardships, I excelled academically and graduated at the top of my high school class. However, at 18, I faced a significant setback when my scholarship was revoked due to my country of origin, despite being assured of a full ride. This setback was especially disheartening because it felt like my hard work had amounted to nothing.

The Challenge: The revocation of my scholarship was a profound personal and professional challenge. It left me feeling worthless and disillusioned as if my efforts had been in vain. The impact was not just emotional but also financial, as I had to navigate a new path under challenging circumstances. Either I went into over $150K in debt for an undergraduate degree or sucked up my ego and attended community college. I decided my ego was not that strong, so I attended community college.

The Turning Point

Defining Moment: The turning point came when I started working as a hostess at a high-end steakhouse. A regular guest, recognizing my potential, suggested I explore a career in human resources. This unexpected encouragement was the catalyst that sparked a change in my approach and mindset. He shared his business card with me and suggested I follow up.

Actions Taken: Embracing this new direction, I reached out to him. Long story, short, while still attending community college I was able to land a full-time role to help me afford my studies. I transitioned into human resources, which led to a successful career. I leveraged every opportunity to learn and grow, ultimately founding my own career and workplace consulting firm, Revamped.

I relied on mentorship, continuous learning, and my growing network to navigate and overcome the challenges I faced.

Lesson Learned

Key Takeaways: The most important lesson I learned is that setbacks can be redirections rather than dead ends. Overcoming adversity taught me resilience, adaptability, and the value of unexpected opportunities. These experiences have shaped me into a more determined and resourceful professional.

Advice for Others: For those facing similar challenges, my advice is to remain open to unexpected opportunities and seek support from mentors and peers. Embrace setbacks as learning experiences and use them as fuel for your journey forward. Persistence and adaptability are key to overcoming obstacles.

Achieving Success

Current Achievements: Today, I am the founder of Revamped, a workplace consulting firm that has helped over 500 professionals. Additionally, I provide over 100K global followers with free resources, insights, remote job postings, and motivation to help them alongside their career strides.

My book of total client salaries exceeds $10M, and I have accumulated over 7 years of HR experience. I also graduated from the University of Virginia with honors graduating debt-free and have worked with leading organizations like American Express and Accenture. These achievements are a testament to the resilience and determination that emerged from my early challenges.

My words and insights have been tapped by leading publications like US World News, Business Insider, CNN, and NPR. I've spoken on panels at Columbia Business School and conferences sponsored by leading tech companies including Google and Microsoft.

Future Goals: Looking ahead, I plan to continue expanding Revamped, helping more professionals achieve their career goals, and contributing positively to the workplace consulting industry. My vision is to inspire and support others in their professional journeys, making a lasting impact on their lives and careers.

I am also studying for the LSAT and GRE to embark on a path towards a JD/MBA as I aspire to transform my consultancy to offer legal council while mastering the essence of building a sustainable business.

Inspiring Others: Be delusional. Believe in your wildest dreams. I encourage people, especially women from underserved communities to reflect on their own challenges and view them as opportunities for growth. No will always mean no if you let it.

Take the first step towards overcoming obstacles by embracing new opportunities and seeking support. Remember, resilience and a positive mindset can transform setbacks into powerful catalysts for success.

Website: www.ariannymercedes.com

Instagram: www.instagram.com/ariannymercedess

Twitter: www.x.com/ariannnyy

LinkedIn: www.linkedin.com/in/arianny

SEPTEMBER 13, 2024

HANNA OLIVAS
CHIEF BRANDING OFFICER
SRS STUDIOS & FENIX TV

FENIX TV EMMYS WEEK

PREMIER GIFTING
Suite

OFFICIAL SPONSORS

 RĒJINS™

Mindfulness: Achieving Balance and Self-Awareness

by Prudence Hatchett

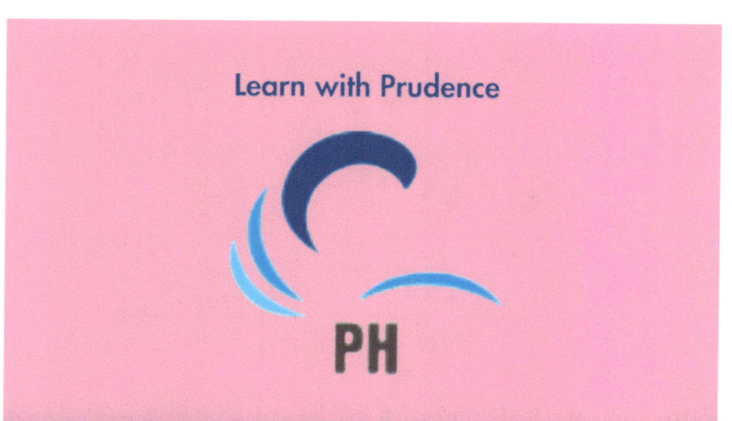

Mindfulness is not just a trend or buzzword, but rather a lifeline for people seeking emotional balance and peace. It's the practice of being present and fully engaged in the moment. In a world that sometimes values popularity over peace or bling over balance, taking care of our mental health is paramount to who we are and who we are to become.

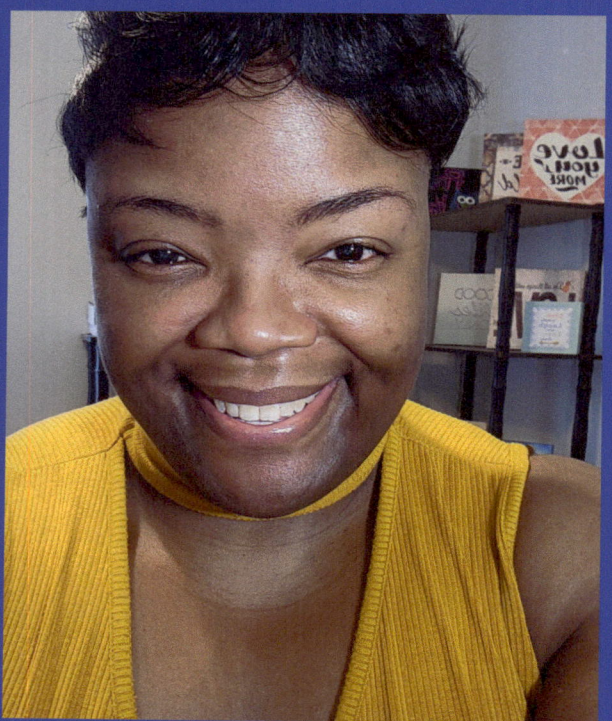

Mindfulness offers a pathway to achieving emotional balance, even while being in the spotlight. This brings me to why I titled the article, "Mindfulness in the Spotlight." I am a champion and advocate for mental wellness, which also includes being a champion for self-confidence. I believe in the importance of discovering your best self so you can live out your authentic self. This means you get to take up the space you are meant to be in and show up in a big way.

But for this to happen, you must be self-aware and mindful of who you are. Showing up for yourself in a big way also means that you feel emotionally balanced and in control of your emotions. When we are in control, we can be fully engaged and present in our environment. This correlates with us being more productive at our craft, more insightful with our knowledge, and more positively impactful to those around us.

Mindfulness can create simplicity and clarity, reduce stress, and improve overall well-being. Some common strategies for mindfulness include deep breathing exercises, meditation, yoga/stretching, counting, positive self-talk, mental tracking, and utilizing positive visualization. Mindfulness is a mental health and wellness strategy that requires consistent practice to be effective.

What does practice mean? Simply put, the word practice means performing an action. It is an action that is performed in a sequence or routine to help gain a more dominant outcome (my own definition). We must manage our mental health by practicing healthy coping skills on a routine basis. Sometimes, it's easy to think that we should only implement the coping skill when experiencing some form of distress that is causing emotional discomfort.

When in fact, we should be practicing coping skills on a routine basis to help train our emotions on how to respond when faced with a challenging stressor. Since we do not have 100% control over our external environment, we will eventually have to confront some form of stressor in life. So, it's not a matter of if the stressor will come, it's a matter of when the stressor will come.

We live in a demanding world where we are all susceptible to emotional distress. Knowing this helps us prepare for the days ahead by equipping ourselves with coping strategies for faster emotional recovery. By consistently practicing mindfulness, we help our mind and body stay in sync, building emotional confidence and ensuring we are always ready to shine in the spotlight.

PH Counseling, LLC
Prudence Hatchett

Get in touch:

PH Counseling, LLC : www.phcounseling.org
Learn with Prudence : learn-with-prudence.myshopify.com
www.facebook.com/phcounselingllc

AUTHOR
Spotlights

From Diagnosis to the Red Carpet:

Hanna Olivas, Chief Branding Officer of She Rises Studios and FENIX TV, Proves Dreams Have No Limits

Hanna Olivas, the powerhouse Chief Branding Officer of She Rises Studios and FENIX TV, is set to make a grand entrance on the red carpet at this year's Emmy Awards, where she will also host the prestigious FENIX TV Premier Gifting Suite for Emmys week. Hanna's journey is a testament to the unyielding spirit of resilience, having turned a terminal diagnosis of rare blood cancer, multiple myeloma, into a mission to inspire women worldwide.

Hanna Olivas's story is one of extraordinary courage and unwavering determination. When diagnosed with multiple myeloma, Hanna chose not to let the terminal illness define her life. Instead, she channeled her will to live into creating She Rises Studios, a groundbreaking platform dedicated to empowering women entrepreneurs, and FENIX TV, an innovative online streaming service.

"Facing a terminal diagnosis made me realize that every moment is precious," said Hanna Olivas. "I wanted to leave a legacy that would inspire women to pursue their dreams, no matter the obstacles."

Hanna's efforts have not gone unnoticed. She has been featured in hundreds of media appearances, including the Today Show, Tamron Hall, People Magazine, and more. Her compelling story and magnetic presence have made her a beacon of hope for countless women striving to overcome their own challenges.

This year, Hanna's journey comes full circle as she walks the red carpet at the Emmys, a symbol of her triumph over adversity. Hosting the FENIX TV Emmys Gifting Suite in Beverly Hills, she brings together Hollywood's elite to celebrate not only the industry's best but also the indomitable human spirit.

Hanna Olivas is a shining example of how dreams can come true regardless of the hurdles life throws at us," said Hanna Olivas, CEO of She Rises Studios. "Her story is an inspiration to all, showing that with passion and perseverance, anything is possible."

Hanna's mission goes beyond business success. Through She Rises Studios and FENIX TV, she aims to create a supportive community for women, providing the resources and encouragement they need to succeed in their entrepreneurial endeavors.

As Hanna graces the Emmy Awards red carpet and hosts the FENIX TV Emmys Gifting Suite, she stands as a living testament to the power of resilience, determination, and the unwavering belief that no diagnosis can define one's destiny.

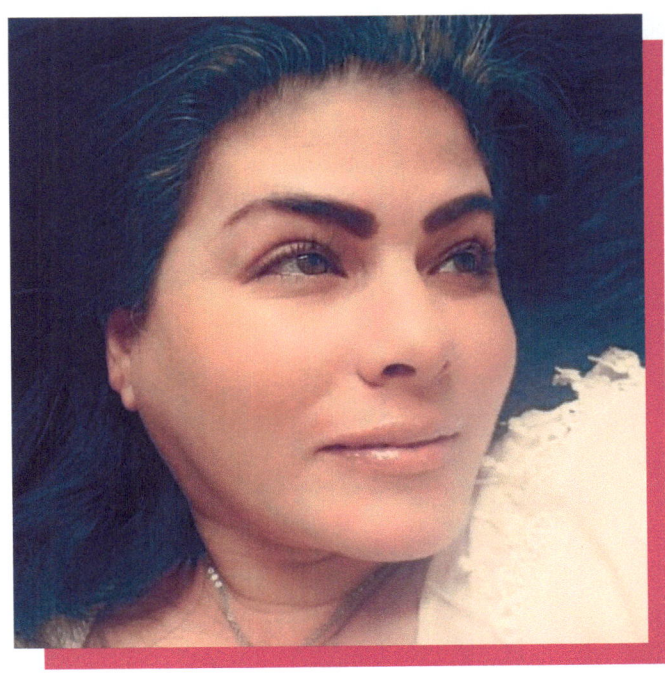

About She Rises Studios

She Rises Studios is a leading platform dedicated to empowering women entrepreneurs through resources, education, and community support. Founded by Hanna Olivas, the studio aims to inspire and elevate women to achieve their fullest potential.

FENIX TV is an innovative online streaming platform that showcases a diverse array of content, focusing on empowerment, inspiration, and education. It is committed to providing a platform for voices that deserve to be heard and stories that need to be told.

About FENIX TV

Hanna Olivas's journey is a powerful reminder that dreams are achievable, no matter the challenges faced along the way. Her story continues to inspire and uplift women around the world, proving that with grit and determination, anything is possible!

www.facebook.com/HannaJOlivas
www.sherisesstudios.com
www.instagram.com/hannaolivasofficial
www.youtube.com/@SheRIsesStudios
www.tiktok.com/@sherisesstudios
www.linkedin.com/in/hanna-olivas-93baa617a

UNSTOPPABLE WOMAN DARES EXECUTIVES TO LEAD WITH A FIERCE HEART

by Merilee Kern, MBA

Relational leadership and management authority Cheryl L. Mason, J.D. is a force of nature. TEDx speaker, author and CEO, Mason his hell bent on helping C-suite executives, senior leaders, companies, and teams develop the skills and tools to lead with authenticity and empathy. As the fourth Presidentially-appointed, Senate-confirmed—and first woman and military spouse—to serve as the CEO/Chairman of the VA Board of Veterans' Appeals prior to starting her own Catalyst Leadership Management business consultancy, Mason is revered for leading with an impactful morale-boosting, people-centric approach—and teaching other managers how to do the same.

Mason brings a unique perspective on adversity and challenges by viewing them as pivotal moments for learning and growth. Additionally, she addresses and highlights the negative impact of invisible "phantom" leaders on the people and the organization. Her consultancy services help CEOs, senior leaders, companies, and teams develop the skills and tools to lead with authenticity and relate with empathy. Mason's mission is to help other business leaders discover and embrace the power of authenticity—being real, caring, relatable, accessible and engaging with each leader's most valuable asset: the people they lead and impact.

As an author and a TEDx speaker, Mason shares insights and stories about people, obstacles, purpose, impact and mindset along with tactical ways leaders can elevate results. Mason is more than a speaker; she's a dynamic force of nature. Her captivating keynote presentations have graced the TEDx stage and have left a profound mark on corporations and nonprofits alike. With her wealth of knowledge, real-world experience, and infectious enthusiasm for leadership, Mason has inspired countless individuals to reach their full potential and take their leadership skills to new heights. She shares her inspiring journey of overcoming life's challenges, while seamlessly incorporating valuable lessons on leadership, vulnerability, and courage. Her ability to connect with business and corporate audiences leaves a lasting impact, empowering others to face adversity with resilience and determination.

Merilee Kern, MBA is an internationally-regarded brand strategist and analyst who reports on noteworthy industry change makers, movers, shakers and innovators across all B2B and B2C categories. Connect with her at LinkedIn www.LinkedIn.com/in/MerileeKern.

In her book, "Dare to Relate: Leading with a Fierce Heart," which emphasizes the significance of cultivating strong relationships within your workforce, Mason shares her journey and unveils her unconventional, yet highly effective approach to leadership.

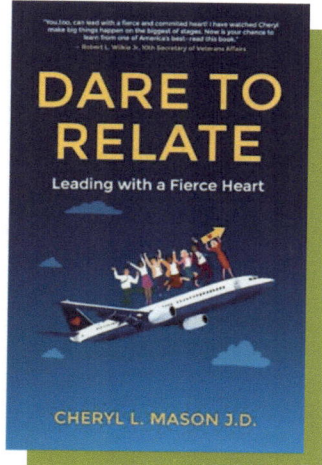

The book highlights how investing time, technology and finances into the employee pool can spur long-term savings substantial bottom line results. The book highlights how relational leadership enhances staff well-being and drives success for leaders and their organizations at large. Through relatable personal stories and insights from her network, Mason's book not only encourages and guides aspirationals to find their own inner leader, but also emphasizes the importance of purposefully impacting the world today and tomorrow.

Mason realized an exceptional career at the Department of Veterans Affairs, beginning as a young attorney and climbing the ranks to eventually become the first woman and military spouse—and senate confirmed—Chairman of the Board of Veterans' Appeals. As the CEO leading over 1200 people serving the veteran and stakeholder communities, she implemented technological innovations to benefit both her employees and customers. Through collaboration with her team, she achieved remarkable results, doubling customer outcomes and increasing morale, retention, and trust. Mason not only successfully grew and managed a large budget but also built and led the most diverse team of people in our history.

With over 30 years of dedicated federal service, coupled with her role as a USAF military spouse, Mason held various challenging positions in the legal and administrative domains. Her accomplishments include establishing an educational program for service members and their families in Germany, managing a diverse range of USAFE support programs encompassing contracts, personnel, budget, and IT, and spearheading a large-scale complex legal operation at the Department of Veterans Affairs (VA). Throughout her career, she has earned a well-deserved reputation as an inspiring leader, placing utmost importance on her team, their families, and the successful accomplishment of their mission.

As Chairman of the Board of Veterans' Appeals at the VA, she led a team of 1200 personnel, including veterans law judges, attorneys, and operations and administrative professionals, and executed a budget of $228 million to meet the Board's mission of conducting hearings and deciding appeals on benefits and services for veterans and their families. As a principal, she advised the Secretary of the VA on diverse matters, from wide-ranging veterans' issues to stakeholder concerns. She implemented revolutionary technological innovations, streamlined processes, and created cost-saving solutions. She improved operations by creating consistency in management practices and championed the investment in personnel by securing more than 65 percent in budget increases over 4 years. She is credited with turning the Board from a dysfunctional organization with low morale and trust and lackluster results into a high-functioning organization, delivering results to veterans and increasing trust and morale in her employees through her people-focused leadership style.

Mason served as Interim Principal Deputy Vice Chairman at the Board of Veterans' Appeals where she was responsible for legislation, regulation, and policy, which included building a diverse political alliance to build consensus with VA leadership, stakeholders and Congress to gain passage of the Veterans Appeals Improvement and Modernization Act of 2017.

Additionally, Mason held a variety of positions, including Deputy Vice Chairman and Veterans Law Judge at the Board, attorney with the Federal Labor Relations Authority, and a Department of the Air Force civilian at HQ United States Air Forces in Europe at Ramstein Air Base, Germany. Mason also served as a contract attorney investigator for the Department of Justice Civil Rights Division specializing in the Americans with Disabilities Act; a military services paralegal coordinator for Europe with Central Texas College; and an instructor at Central Texas College, Kapaun Air Station, Germany.

She also served as a PREVENTS Task Force Ambassador, along with Lead Ambassador Second Lady Karen Pence. PREVENTS was the first national public health campaign to address suicide prevention. Mason also worked closely with First Lady Dr. Jill Biden's Joining Forces initiative to address the challenges and issues of military and veteran families.

In recognition of her fierce commitment and actions around military spouse employment and transitioning veterans, Mason received the Hiring Our Heroes 2022 Bonnie Amos Lifetime Achievement Impact Award from the US Chamber of Commerce. Mason was recognized by Disabled American Veterans as the 2021 Outstanding Federal Executive and received the FedHealthIT 2020 Leading for Impact: Women in Leadership Award.

Mason's extraordinary journey stands as a testament to her unwavering dedication and exceptional leadership prowess. Being a catalyst leader involves facing challenges, overcoming obstacles, and genuinely caring for and supporting your employees.

A Haunting with a Twist

Who would build a house purposely to be haunted?

100 people have perished or gone missing over three decades. Now two paranormal research teams enter to solve the mystery. But first they must learn to work together if they want to survive Blood Mansion.

"I did enjoy it -- especially after they all got to the house. I thought there was good tension and I found it rather spooky -- or at least as spooky as someone like me could find that sort of story. But, yeah, I was into it and rooting for the good guys!

I did smile a few times at the skeptical investigators and recognized some of our attitudes and techniques. Other times I thought to myself, 'If we'd seen that, I might have a different attitude!'"

James Underdown
Renowned Paranormal Investigator

"Wow! 'Blood Mansion' is an electrifying journey through the shadows of destiny and the complexities of morality."

Kate Milly
May 12, 2024

 www.storywriter.ca

Jamie O'Neill

The Writer Behind Journey of My Soul, a Guided Journal

Jamie O'Neill has established herself as a distinctive voice in the world of guided journaling & intuitive healing, bringing a unique blend of introspection and inspiration to her readers. With her book Journey of My Soul, O'Neill invites individuals on a transformative journey, encouraging deep reflection and personal growth.

From an early age, O'Neill exhibited a profound curiosity about the human experience. Her passion for understanding the intricacies of the mind and soul led her to explore various disciplines, including psychology, metaphysics, spirituality, and creative writing. This diverse background is evident in her work, where she seamlessly blends these elements to create a holistic approach to self-discovery.

Journey of My Soul is more than just a journal; it is a companion for those seeking to explore their inner landscapes. O'Neill designed this guided journal with a series of thought-provoking prompts, reflective exercises, and inspirational quotes that help readers navigate their emotions, aspirations, and challenges. Each page is crafted to encourage introspection, fostering a deeper connection with oneself.

O'Neill's writing style is both gentle and profound, offering readers a safe space to explore their innermost thoughts. Her empathy and understanding of the human condition shine through in every prompt, making the journaling process a nurturing and enlightening experience. This approach has resonated with many, earning her a dedicated following of readers who find solace and guidance in her words.

One of the standout features of "Journey of My Soul" is its emphasis on mindfulness. O'Neill encourages readers to be present in the moment, to appreciate the beauty of their journey, and to embrace the lessons that each experience brings. This mindful approach not only enhances the journaling experience but also cultivates a greater sense of peace and clarity in everyday life.

O'Neill's inspiration to write "Journey of My Soul" stemmed from her own healing journey of overcoming alcoholism. Through her struggles and triumphs, she discovered the power of introspection and self-love, and she now aims to be a beacon of light for others battling addiction. Her personal experiences imbue her work with authenticity and compassion, offering readers genuine support and encouragement on their paths to recovery.

Beyond her work as an author, O'Neill is also renowned for her tarot and oracle readings, as well as her one-on-one spiritual development coaching. These services provide her clients with personalized insights and guidance, helping them to navigate their spiritual paths with greater confidence and clarity. Her intuitive abilities and compassionate approach make her a sought-after spiritual advisor, complementing the wisdom found in her written work.

In an era where self-care and mental well-being are more important than ever, Jamie O'Neill's "Journey of My Soul" stands out as a beacon of light. Her work reminds us that the path to understanding ourselves is a continuous journey, one that requires patience, compassion, and a willingness to explore the depths of our soul. Through her guided journal, O'Neill offers readers the guidance and inspiration needed to embark on this transformative path, making her a cherished figure in the realm of personal development.

 www.amazon.com/Journey-My-Soul-Guided-Journal/dp/B0CJD8B9LC

 www.silvermoonoracle.com

UNLOCKING YOUR ENTREPRENEURIAL POTENTIAL: INSIGHTS FROM THE AUTHORS OF 'DARE TO DREAM BIG'

In a world where dreams can seem out of reach, seven visionary authors have crafted "Dare to Dream Big," a guide that challenges the status quo. Focusing on innovation, scaling, and business success, this book offers a roadmap for entrepreneurs and business leaders. More than a guide, it's a movement inspiring people to aim high. In this exclusive feature, we interview the authors behind this transformative book, exploring their insights, challenges, and experiences.

Darlene Oliver
mompreneurssweetspot.com

Joahna Tupas
schoolinabackpack.com

Klara Reid
lifeandpassiionredefined.com

What sparked the idea for your chapter; why did you choose to collaborate on this book?

In Dare To Dream Big, I wrote about "Becoming a NOISE-maker," with NOISE standing for a Narrative Of Inspiration, Strength, and Encouragement. After a second bout of heart failure, I questioned sharing this message while sick, but felt God's assurance: "Your message will be even stronger." Writing with just 18% heart function and a defibrillator LifeVest™, I lived and proved my message.

— Edwina Adams

The idea for my chapter, "Courage to Begin Again," was to honor my dad's lifelong courage. His entrepreneurial spirit and focus on innovation and mentoring, especially of the younger generation (including myself), were truly inspiring. Writing it was tough after his sudden passing, but it was a way to share his legacy of success, stories, and lessons, ensuring his spirit continues to inspire.

— Joahna Tupas

In my journey through entrepreneurship, I've come to realize that true success isn't just about reaching your goals—it's about the impact you make along the way. 'Dare to Dream Big' isn't just a book; it's a testament to the resilience and creativity that drive us forward, no matter the obstacles. As I reflect on my own path, I see that embracing every challenge as an opportunity has not only shaped my business but also enriched my life. This book is a celebration of that journey, offering insights and inspiration for anyone ready to turn their dreams into reality.

— Adriana Luna Carlos

Can you provide an example of how applying a principle from 'Dare to Dream Big' resulted in a significant breakthrough in your business?

Embark on a transformative journey where impostor syndrome serves as fuel to achieve your wildest dreams. Overcoming self-doubt led Gemma Bulos on a quest to realize unimaginable feats: mobilizing an unprecedented global peace movement, speaking at the UN, teaching at Stanford, and bringing clean water to millions. Each victory magnifies how embracing our true power and redefining our unique narrative ignites limitless potential.

— Gemma Bulos

Self-expression" necessitates the ability to lose oneself in the pursuit of goals that are secondary to oneself. This one idea from "Dare to Dream Big" served as the focal point of my company! Here, I seized my feminine energy, assumed leadership roles, and used my V.O.I.C.E. to write the next chapter of my life. My personal story's final missing puzzle piece led to this epiphany.

— Elizzabeth Coreyy

What guidance would you offer to aspiring entrepreneurs facing challenges in innovating and scaling their businesses in today's competitive environment?

If innovation is challenging, research what customers are saying, understand their needs and evolve or adapt your offerings accordingly. Every challenge is an opportunity to learn and grow. I've had to evolve countless times; I expect it now like the change of seasons. That's how I ended up offering over 15 services nationwide. Remember, it's always about your customers. Never remain stagnant.

— Darlene Oliver

Life has many surprises... good and bad ones. From these, you build the best life you can. At times, the hardest to take are the ones that make you the person you should be. After you succeed, you give back, and the blessing starts. You arrived. I love where I got through the fight of my life. If it was to start again, I would do the same.

— Klara Reid

As we conclude, it becomes evident that "Dare to Dream Big" is more than a guide; it's a catalyst for business innovation and growth. The authors' passion and dedication shine through every page, making it a must-read for anyone looking to transform their dreams into reality. To embark on your own journey of entrepreneurial success, you can purchase "Dare to Dream Big" on Amazon.com. Don't miss out on this invaluable resource!

www.sherisesstudios.com
www.amazon.com/dp/1960136763
www.amazon.ca/dp/1960136763

Embracing Resilience:
MY JOURNEY FROM ASSAULT TO AUDACITY

My name is Michele Paiva; I am autistic (she/her) and a therapist --and like many readers; I am a survivor of assault, neglect, abuse and loss. Like many readers, I also had the audacity to heal. It's a process and path I am still on.

My journey into the world of financial therapy is deeply intertwined with professional and, my personal experiences.

Before facing significant adversity, my life, like many others, had its share of trials and triumphs. In my early twenties, I was filled with hope and ambition, but a traumatic event would soon alter the course of my life.

I was (sexually) assaulted, left for dead, and underwent emergency surgery to save my life. This harrowing experience shattered me physically, emotionally and financially. I didn't realize then that trauma could have such a profound impact on one's economic well-being.

The Challenge

The trauma I endured left me not only emotionally scarred but financially devastated. The financial strain, coupled with the physical healing, scars that were a reminder and the emotional aftermath, was overwhelming. I was broken in ways I never anticipated, struggling to piece my life back together.

A decade later, my world was further upended when I held my mother, my best friend, as she succumbed to cancer. I had to find the strength to tell her it was okay to let go of her suffering. This moment of profound grief and responsibility was the hardest thing I've ever faced, but it also became a pivotal point in my life.

The Turning Point

The passing of my mother and the profound challenges I faced catalyzed a profound shift in my perspective.

I realized that I didn't want others to endure the silent suffering I experienced or to face financial hardship without understanding the connection between trauma and finances.

This realization was the spark that ignited my transformation. I decided to channel my experiences into something meaningful, leading me to pursue a path in financial therapy.

So much about women is taboo; we are often taught that it isn't ladylike to talk about menstruation, menopause, our assaults or struggles, including financial struggles.

Actions Taken

To address and overcome my challenges, I embarked on a journey of healing and self-discovery. Part of that was being my authentic self; letting my autism be unmasked. Not trying to fit in. It was liberating and I think everyone should let their weird fly as much as possible.

I pursued transpersonal psychology, which combines spiritual and psychological insights, to understand and address the trauma that had impacted my life and finances as well as other women.

I had a career that taught me how women hold so much inside, and suffer in silence. I immersed myself in studying financial literacy and therapy, driven by a desire to help others who faced similar struggles. I wrote three books on financial therapy, sharing my insights and experiences. Additionally, I created the first and only financial therapy app, aiming to provide a unique resource for those seeking to navigate their financial and emotional challenges.

Lessons Learned

My journey taught me that resilience and recovery are not just about overcoming adversity but also about understanding and addressing the underlying issues.

I learned that trauma can profoundly affect financial stability and that healing involves both emotional and practical strategies.

Overcoming these challenges changed me deeply, shaping my approach as a therapist and my commitment to supporting others.

One of the most important lessons is that healing is a spectrum; we may not all be on the autism spectrum, but we are all on a spectrum of healing and overcoming.

Even my physical scars are gone; I was told I would never have children but I did have two. I needed a C-section with my first. My scars were gone because a wonderful OB/GYN when I had that surgical birth, with my daughter, cut the scars away; I didn't know until I woke up that she did this for me.

She had the audacity to heal parts of me that were holding me back, beyond my control- but within hers; and I am forever grateful.

I learned to let go, and use that space as a pivot to create meaningful change, after many tears of course- and sometimes those tears of loss still leak-- but they water and nourish my mission.

Advice for Others

For those facing similar challenges, remember that your journey is unique, and healing takes time. Seek support from professionals who understand the intersection of trauma and financial struggles. Embrace resources and strategies that resonate with you, whether it's therapy, financial education, or self-care practices. Most importantly, be kind to yourself

and acknowledge your progress, no matter how small. While I do not wish pain on anyone, if you have it, remember it is an energy and energy can change form. You are more powerful than you can imagine.

Achieving Success

Today, I am proud of the successes I've achieved despite the obstacles I faced. I think my late mother would be proud of me. It is a homage to her. My work as a financial therapist has allowed me to help others understand and overcome their financial and emotional difficulties. The creation of my app and my books are testaments to the power of resilience and the importance of addressing trauma's impact on financial health. My experiences have fueled my passion for helping others, and I continue to thrive by focusing on my mission to support those in need. Don't be shy about your success. You were meant for greatness.

Future Goals

I expect life will get tough and knock me down a few times; but looking ahead, I aspire to expand my reach and impact through continued innovation in financial therapy. I aim to further develop resources that support individuals in navigating their financial and emotional landscapes. My goal is to inspire and empower more people to find their path to emotional healing and financial stability.

To anyone facing their own challenges, I encourage you to reflect on your journey and seek the support you need. Embrace the lessons you learn along the way and remember that your resilience is a powerful force. Take the first step toward overcoming your obstacles and building a future where you can thrive. Your story is unique, and with the right support and mindset, you can turn assaults to your mind or body into an audacious comeback. Feel free to connect with me at TheFinanceTherapist.com

I am an autistic psychotherapist (she/her) who specializes in financial therapy and trauma. I am far-too fond of 80's sitcoms, watercolor painting, tofu and raising monarch butterflies for release in my spare time.

SEPTEMBER 13, 2024

SHE RISES STUDIOS   FENIX TV

SAVANNAH KENNICK
ACTRESS

CHRIS BEAL
CO-PRODUCER, EMMY NOMINATED
SERIES, PEACOCK'S, "BEL AIR"

ROCKET MINJIZZLE
CELEBRITY MAKEUP ARTIST/
INFLUENCER & RED CARPET
CORRESPONDENT

DANA HICKS-HUNGERFORD
ACTRESS AND DESIGNER

KIKI SHEPARD
ACTRESS, BOUNCE TV'S,
"MIND YOUR BUSINESS"/
TV PERSONALITY/PHILANTHROPIST

ARELI MADRIGAL
SOCAL LATINA LIFESTYLE/BEAUTY
CONTENT CREATOR/INFLUENCER

GABRIELLE REECE
VOLLEYBALL PLAYER, SPORTS
ANNOUNCER, FASHION MODEL,
ACTRESS AND PRODUCER

FENIX TV EMMYS WEEK

PREMIER GIFTING
Suite

RISING STRONG:
My Journey from Survival to Success

My name is Jennifer Johnson and I am the owner of True Fashionistas, the largest lifestyle resale store in Florida.

I grew up on a farm in central Minnesota the 2nd oldest of 6 siblings. My dad showed me and my siblings what hard work was like. He worked tirelessly to put food on our table and make ends meet for my family.

My last year in high school I met a boy whom I began dating. He seemed great at first until he started hitting me, abusing me verbally. I didn't know that the hitting and verbal abuse would be the least of my issues. The physical violence turned into sexual violence with him raping me. I didn't matter that I said no he would continue each and every time. The violence also got worse. It got so bad that when I graduated and was going on to college on a scholarship for broadcast communications (I wanted to be a TV news anchor so bad) he threatened to kill me if I ended up going. I never went to college because I was so scared.

The turning point was one night he drove me off the road and tried to kill me. Something changed in me that night. Something just clicked and I realized this is not how I want to live my life. I feel it was as though God was talking to me saying get out now while you are still alive. It was by that grace of God that I did get out. Over the course of the next few months I was able to distance myself from him, get a restraining order and take my life back. This was something I really did on my own because I didn't want anyone to think less of me or not believe me. It was a very tough time but I drew on my faith (even though I didn't understand it at the time) to get me through.

This entire experience changed me. At the time I thought it was terrible, and it was, but now 30+ years later reflecting on this entire experience I learned so much about myself and about resilience. Your past becomes part of the fabric that you are today. You use your past to change you future and to make your future even better.

I realize that no matter what you are facing there will be light at the end of the tunnel and things in life happen FOR you not TO you! The reason all of this happened to me was so that now, later in life, I am able to go out and speak to people and motivate them and I do just that. From small stages to large stages to intimate events. I speak about what happened to me, how I got out and what I am doing with what happened to me now. f I can help just ONE person then what I went through was all worth it.

I harnessed all that negativity, violence and pain and went on to become Ms. Petite MN, a model and actress and advocate for stopping sexual violence.

I am now an entrepreneur (I owe 3 different companies) as well as an author, small business coach and professional speaker. I use all that life has thrown at me and use it to encourage others.

My goal is to continue speaking in front of audiences world wide to spread the voice of encouragement, resilience and hope.

I invite each of you to look at your own life and the challenges that you have faced along the way. What have they taught you? What were the lessons, as there always lessons in everything that happens for us. It is our job to find out what those lessons are, learn from them and teach them to others so it can better their lives.

I didn't allow the challenges of my past to hold me down. I took the challenges of my past and harnessed them to create a better future for myself I used them to propel me to become UNSTOPPABLE!

Jennifer Ann Johnson

From national model to founder of a successful resale empire, Jennifer Johnson embodies entrepreneurial grit and grace. As the visionary behind True Fashionistas, Florida's largest lifestyle resale store, she's mastered building a thriving business while maintaining personal well-being. Her Amazon bestseller and award-winning podcast offer a blueprint for success that resonates with business owners everywhere.

Jennifer's impact extends far beyond her own achievements. As a coach and speaker, she's transformed countless entrepreneurs' lives through her online academy and coaching programs. Her expertise, featured in Forbes and Vogue, coupled with her dynamic presence from national TV appearances, captivates and inspires action.

Recognized as a Gulfshore Life Businesswoman of the Year, Jennifer doesn't just teach success – she embodies it. Her blend of experience, strategies, and motivational energy empowers audiences to achieve their dreams.

Facebook: www.facebook.com/profile.php?id=100089312054101&mibextid=LQQJ4d
Instagram: Jennifer.ann_johnson
Linkedin: www.linkedin.com/in/jennifer-johnson-39237448
True FashionistasFacebook: www.facebook.com/truefashionistasresale/
Instagram: truefashionistasresale

FROM MUMBAI TO MILLIONAIRE: MY JOURNEY OF RESILIENCE AND REINVENTION

Growing up in Mumbai, India, I was immersed in the city's relentless hustle and vibrant vitality. My parents' sacrifices were the foundation of my aspirations, as I was raised in a middle-class family. Their unwavering support enabled me to relocate to the United States in order to pursue my aspiration of establishing my own business and pursuing higher education. I was aware that I required a distinct environment to transform my entrepreneurial aspirations into a reality after encountering the bureaucratic and unethical practices in India.

The year 2010 marked a significant turning point in my existence. I held a secure position as the Vice President of Product Management at a major corporation, and my wife and I were expecting our first child. My wife encouraged me to establish my own business, as she was aware that if I did not act now, I may never achieve it. I established my company with her assistance, motivated by pioneering concepts regarding video interview technology that were ahead of their time.

The initial year was exceedingly difficult. Due to my existing connections, acquiring my initial client was relatively straightforward; however, attracting subsequent clients proved to be a more challenging endeavor. I experienced a decline in my professional identity as I transitioned from the role of VP of Product Management to that of a recruiter. I found this change to be difficult to accept, and I encountered difficulties with the brand's perception. At times, I entertained the idea of resigning and returning to my corporate career.

The pivotal moment occurred when I elected to collaborate with a coach who introduced me to the concept of "burning the bridge," which involved eliminating the safety net that bound me to my previous identity. My perspective changed as soon as I relinquished that rope. I accepted my new position and concentrated on becoming the most effective recruiter possible. My company experienced accelerated growth as a result of our ability to differentiate our services and refine our business practices. We achieved a $1 million revenue within three years, and by 2015, we had multiplied it.

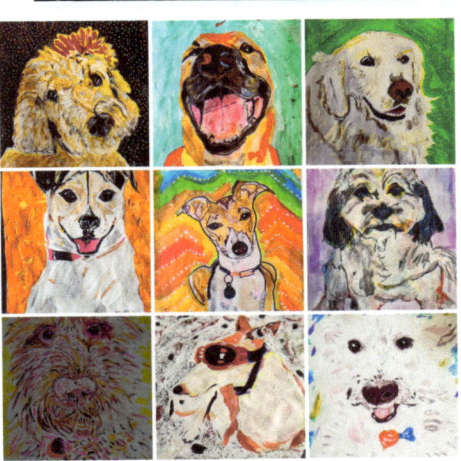

The oil and gas industry experienced a subsequent collapse, which resulted in numerous companies losing their footing. We reacted to the downturn by pivoting. Our revenue increased by another million as we examined new industries and established a consulting division. Our capacity to pivot and adapt became our most significant asset, enabling us to persist in our growth despite the obstacles.

My personal and professional life have been significantly altered as a result of my ability to surmount these challenges. I have acquired an understanding of the significance of adaptability, resilience, and the ability to embrace change. Burning the bridge was an essential lesson that compelled me to perpetually innovate and commit fully.

I recommend that those who are confronted with comparable obstacles embrace change and relinquish the safety nets that constrain them. Obtain assistance from mentors or coaches and concentrate on setting yourself apart in your profession. Your greatest allies are adaptability and resilience. No matter how insurmountable the challenges may appear, have faith in your capacity to adapt and develop.

Presently, the following accomplishments have: My company is currently flourishing, and our transition from a small startup to a multi-million-dollar enterprise is a testament to our innovation and resilience. Our success has been significantly influenced by our capacity to pivot, and we have established a reputation for excellence in our field.

I aspire to continue to have a positive influence in the future. I intend to broaden our offerings, investigate new markets, and enhance our innovation. In addition to my professional pursuits, I derive satisfaction and significance from contributing to others. Painting portraits of deceased canines is one method I employ to provide solace to their families. This practice is soul-nourishing, bringing pleasure to others and providing me with a sense of fulfillment.

Consider your obstacles and determine how you can incorporate these teachings into your personal life. Embrace change, seek assistance, and do not hesitate to destroy the bridge that hinders your progress. Begin the process of surmounting your challenges and achieving an unstoppable status. Incredible success and growth can result from your voyage, regardless of its challenges.

ABHIJEET NARVEKAR

Abhi, originally from Mumbai, moved to the USA for his Master's in Industrial Engineering. In 2010, he founded his company, which has been recognized as one of the Fastest Growing Alumni companies from Oklahoma State University and has won multiple Best Places to Work awards. Passionate about helping others, Abhi's impact is captured in testimonials like, "Abhi changed my life!" His dedication to creating a supportive and dynamic workplace is the cornerstone of his success.

www.thefervidgroup.com
www.careerunleashed.com
www.linkedin.com/in/abhijeetnarvekar

by Ashleigh Netter

BETTING ON YOURSELF: NAVIGATING LIFE'S STORMS FOR AUTHENTIC SUCCESS

Imagine having everything in place: a stable job, a supportive family, and a bright future. Now imagine losing all of that within 24 hours. How would you feel? Devastated? Confused? Angry? Afraid?

I've felt all of these emotions, but most of all, I've felt numb. Life's storms—whether personal, professional, or environmental—can dismantle everything we've worked for in an instant.

For me, it was on August 29, 2005, when Hurricane Katrina hit New Orleans, Louisiana, with unprecedented force. I went from an aspiring pharmacist student to a survivor navigating the chaos the storm left behind.

The Turning Point

Life's unpredictability shook me to my core, leaving me feeling like I was navigating a storm without a compass. The idea of betting on myself seemed like a gamble, but in this moment it was the most empowering choice I could make. Instead of succumbing to the chaos, I chose to take risks, embrace challenges, and transform my life and career. This encounter sparked the creation of my life's mission: Living to Inspire and Transform (LIT).

***Risk #1:** GET L.I.T.! I must live to inspire and transform in everything I do.*

Embracing Life's Storms

Life's storms bring challenges, but instead of avoiding them, embrace them. Each storm teaches us resilience, determination, big-picture thinking, and emotional intelligence. These qualities become our assets —our capital gains. Embrace your storms, own them, and leverage the lessons they provide.

Principle 1: Embrace the Challenge

Every storm, whether a personal setback, a career obstacle, or a financial crisis, comes with its own set of challenges. Embrace these challenges rather than avoiding them. They teach us resilience, determination, and the ability to see the bigger picture. These qualities become your capital gains—valuable assets that you can leverage for authentic success.

Principle 2: Inspire Through Your Journey

Authentic success isn't just about personal achievement; it's about inspiring others. Listen and reflect before responding. This practice allows you to check your emotional capacity and respond effectively. When you find yourself in others' stories and build genuine connections, you not only inspire hope but also create a supportive network.

Principle 3: Transform with Gratitude

Practice daily gratitude, especially for the storms. Gratitude transforms every area of life, fostering an environment of kindness, respect, and support. This mindset benefits you and those around you, creating a community of growth and support.

Betting on Yourself

Betting on oneself means taking risks and embracing the unknown with confidence. It's about believing in your ability to overcome obstacles and turn challenges into opportunities.

Here's how you can do it:

- **Acknowledge Your Strengths:** Recognize and celebrate your abilities and achievements. This boosts your confidence and prepares you to face new challenges.
- **Set Clear Goals:** Define what success means to you. Set realistic and achievable goals that align with your values and aspirations.

- **Take Calculated Risks:** Step out of your comfort zone and take risks that can lead to growth. Assess the potential outcomes and make informed decisions.
- **Learn from Failures:** View failures as learning opportunities. Analyze what went wrong, learn from it, and apply those lessons to future endeavors.
- **Seek Support:** Surround yourself with supportive individuals who believe in your vision. Their encouragement can provide the motivation needed to keep moving forward.

The Impact of Betting on Yourself

Applying these principles can significantly impact your life and community. Through leadership and influence, you can secure opportunities, create initiatives, and support those in need.

For example, I've been able to secure over $1.5 million in corporate dollars to establish scholarship programs, feed thousands of families, and launch initiatives that provide essential services to underserved communities.

This isn't a flex; it's a testament to what betting on yourself and being L.I.T. can achieve.

My story is a powerful reminder that we all can rise from our personal Katrinas. As you reflect on your life, consider where you can take the risk to bet on yourself. What areas of your life are ripe for change? What dreams have you been putting off because of fear or uncertainty? Now is the time to act. Whether it's starting a new career, launching a business, or pursuing a personal passion, take that leap of faith.

Ask yourself: What do I have to lose? More importantly, what do I have to gain? Success on social media and trending topics often stem from those who dared to bet on themselves. They share their journeys, their failures, and their victories, inspiring others to do the same.

So, share your story. Document your journey. Let your experience inspire others. Use hashtags like #BetOnYourself, #TakeTheRisk, #GetLIT and #AuthenticSuccess to connect with a community of risk-takers and dream-chasers.

My challenge to you is to show up every day betting on yourself. Take risks, embrace your storms, and inspire and transform those around you.

My name is Dr. Ashleigh Netter, and I believe in betting on myself for authentic success. Connect with me on ashleighnetter.com, LinkedIn, Instagram, and YouTube.

Stuck in a rut? Craving a life makeover? Feeling a bit off-kilter?

GUIDED JOURNEY COACHING
1:1 MENTORSHIP
With
Pauline Grouette

JSCS Certified Coach

Author

Vision Board Facilitator

Go from **Accountability** to *Abundance*

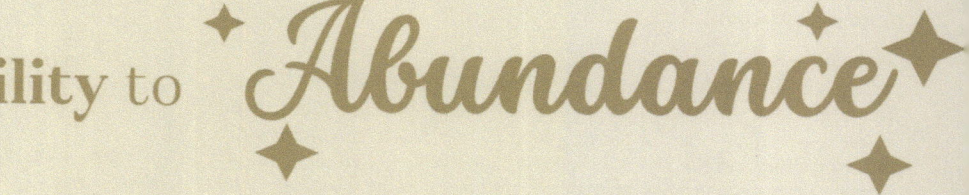

Guided Journey
Coaching & Consulting

by Christina Collura

AUTISM ADVOCACY TO ENTREPRENEURIAL SUCCESS

"If they can't learn the way we teach – maybe we should teach they way we learn".

A quote that I always lived by and it became even more apparent after my son's Autism diagnosis. My name is Christina Collura, I am a mom of two boys, a full-time educator, turned Autism advocate and award-winning entrepreneur. I was married for almost 12 years and in that time, faced the most challenging realization – my youngest son is Autistic. In that time, I was also dealing with Stage 4 endometriosis which required extensive surgery to even be able to tackle the ups and downs with my son's diagnosis and of course, my own life, insecurities and anxiety.

With Luca (my son's) diagnosis came the "AH-HA" moment, and a turning point that went back to the very quote that you read at the beginning. Luca's diagnosis wasn't going to be a barrier, but simply a leaning curve for everyone that he encountered- figuring out how he needed to learn. This completely changed my mentality both professional and personally and made the quote even more blinding!

Luca loved the texture and using chalk as a catalyst for colouring, scribbling etc.He could spend all day scribbling and doodling on my driveway. I decided to put that interest to good use and apply it to a wooden name puzzle. I hand painted a chalkboard base to the indented spaces of the puzzle – and watched his fine motor skills develop – with not being able to go "out of the lines" as he wrote the letters in his name L-u-c-a. 4 weeks later – this spiraled onto paper and my mind was blown! How did I just come up with an idea to help my son to learn to successfully write his name?

I took this idea – literally googled a manufacturer overseas (who turned out to be one of the biggest in China), got a prototype made for and Uppercase and Numbers 1-20 puzzle (with a chalkboard base) and brought the successful concept into my Kindergarten classroom and saw the same success!! The difference was – many other children – both on and off the spectrum – wanted to play!! An inclusive product concept that just brough children of all needs and abilities together!Did I just do this? Facing my own obstacles, demons, fears, I took the idea and ran with it. We are currently a fast-growing brand with a patented concept that is reaching more and more children, while advocating and spreading inclusivity along the way.

Throughout this process, I continue to look back and realize that I am the only one that could have made this happen. People often ask me "how did I get here?".My response is always "one day at a time". That stands true with battling the challenges of Autism everyday! I continue to learn and grow with my son – one day at a time.

Being named Top 100 Inspirational Woman through my work with Autism Awareness, An RBC Woman of Influence Nominee, Mom's Choice Award Winner, Parent's Pick Award Winner, Total Mom Pitch Top 100 (to name a few) – I continue to have pinch me moments – but the reality is – it all comes back to the one decision I made after my son's diagnosis – to figure out how he needed to learn! That was the most important decision I made with that tough diagnosis.

I inspire all woman out there to make the best possible decision for both you and your family. Forget about what everyone else is going to think – and decide your own path and go for it!You'll never be disappointed for trying – you'll be more disappointed for not!

Becoming a successful entrepreneur while raising an autistic child requires resilience, adaptability, and a unique set of skills. Here are some key ideas that I continue to draw upon from such a journey

RESILIENCE AND PERSEVERANCE

- **Never Give Up:** The journey is filled with challenges, from balancing parenting responsibilities with business demands to overcoming societal stigma. Resilience is key.

- **Embrace Failures:** Viewing setbacks as learning opportunities rather than failures can propel growth and improvement.

TIME MANAGEMENT AND PRIORITIZATION

- **Effective Time Management:** Balancing business and personal responsibilities requires meticulous planning and prioritization.
- **Delegation:** Learning to delegate tasks in business and seeking support in parenting (e.g., from family, friends, or professional caregivers) is crucial.

ADAPTABILITY AND FLEXIBILITY

- **Stay Adaptable:** Both business and parenting can be unpredictable. Being flexible and adaptable helps in navigating sudden changes and challenges.
- **Creative Problem-Solving:** Finding creative solutions for both business hurdles and parenting challenges can make a significant difference.

ADVOCACY AND AWARENESS

- **Raise Awareness:** Being an advocate for autism awareness can create a supportive community and potentially open business opportunities.
- **Network and Connect:** Building a strong network of other parents, professionals, and business connections can provide emotional support and practical advice.

SELF-CARE AND MENTAL HEALTH

- **Prioritize Self-Care:** Taking care of oneself is crucial to avoid burnout. This includes finding time for rest, hobbies, and mental health care.
- **Seek Professional Help:** Therapy or counseling can provide support for managing stress and maintaining mental well-being.

FINANCIAL MANAGEMENT

- **Smart Financial Planning:** Careful financial planning and budgeting are essential to manage both business expenses and the costs associated with raising a child with special needs.
- **Seek Funding and Grants:** Exploring available funding, grants, or financial aid for both business and autism-related needs can provide additional support.

EDUCATION AND LEARNING

- **Continuous Learning:** Keeping up with both business trends and the latest in autism research and therapies can provide valuable insights and strategies.
- **Leverage Resources:** Utilizing available resources such as online courses, support groups, and business mentorship programs can aid in personal and professional growth.

EMPATHY AND COMPASSION

- **Empathetic Leadership:** Leading with empathy and understanding can create a positive work environment and build strong relationships with clients and employees.
- **Teaching Inclusivity:** Promoting inclusivity and understanding within the business can set a positive example and create a supportive community.

CELEBRATING SMALL WINS

- **Celebrate Milestones:** Recognizing and celebrating small victories, both in business and personal life, can boost morale and provide motivation to keep going.
- **Practice Gratitude:** Maintaining a positive outlook and practicing gratitude can improve overall well-being and provide a sense of accomplishment.

You really are your own worst critique; but I also know I have one (two) sweet boys that need my drive and dedication! I need it too! You can and will do it – you just need to put your mind to it to become the most "unstoppable" version of yourself!

Christina

Christina Collura
Full Time Educator of 20 years
CEO AND FOUNDER – Creative Beginning

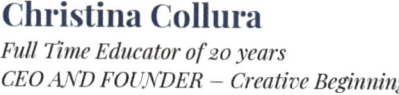

www.creativebeginning.ca
www.facebook.com/creativebeginning
www.instagram.com/creativebeginning

by Darlene Taylor

CULTIVATING STRENGTH, SELF-LOVE, AND A PURPOSE-FILLED PATH THROUGH ADVERSITY

Having to endure one life-altering-do-over after another has forged the courage to face whatever comes my way as I know that I have cultivated the strength of character and self-love to weather any storm that may shift its winds my way. Several years ago, I abandoned my career, divorced, and became wholeheartedly focused on my role as a mother. All those life-altering changes sent me on a self-discovery path over the next few years, which morphed into the opportunity of a lifetime to explore and define myself.

MY JOURNEY

I was always a dedicated student to whom academic success was extremely important. I decided to become a therapist at age 14 and never looked back, working hard toward that goal and holding tightly to the idea that a successful career was the most important achievement I could attain. I earned a Master's in Social Work, nurturing a dream to change the world, one family at a time. I focused intently on my career, taking for granted that I would easily fall into the traditional cycle of life - find a husband and have a family.

Naively, I created a plan in my head during graduate school that laid out precisely how adulthood would unfold, but by graduation, I felt behind schedule and pressured to make my current relationship official - despite signs it wasn't the right fit. Determined to cram my life into the box I built, I got married at 28 to someone whose career became the center of our lives and forced me and my career into the back seat.

As a coach's wife, my main priority was to support his career. I still held fast to my career dreams, but whenever I began to gain traction, we had to relocate. Multiple moves meant that I couldn't secure licensure to work as a therapist in each different state, so I eventually switched to teaching and became a professor at The University of Cincinnati. With every move, I began losing myself and focusing more on being the "coach's wife" while my dreams drifted out of focus. Once our daughter was born, my focus turned to being a great mother and I soon lost myself in that role, too.

MY TURNING POINT

Then the biggest "do-over" of all happened - divorce. I had to figure out who I was now and what I wanted the rest of my life to look like. It was clear that going back to my previous career and ideas of success no longer made sense. Life had changed me and I accepted that it was okay to reinvent myself based on my ever-changing circumstances. I now had a responsibility to think about the kind of woman I wanted to model for my daughter and to find the courage to make choices that were authentic to the best version of me. My decision to get a divorce meant giving up everything that I thought embodied success and finding a different path while finding the confidence to believe in myself again. It meant that I had to resurrect my career and decide what being a successful woman and mother would look like. I could let go of everyone else's opinions and finally decide and define what I wanted for myself.

LESSONS LEARNED

Some of the most valuable lessons I learned were:
- ➤ It's never too late to start over
- ➤ Be fearless
- ➤ Let go of the need for the validation of others

The most important thing I did was repair my relationship with the idea of being selfish. I had to embrace that the only way to be successful was to ensure that I was doing the best job of nurturing myself by understanding the true meaning of self-care. I immediately started therapy and medication to deal with the depression that had hampered my ability to

my confidence and get back into the work world. Caring for myself became my priority. I took control of my health focusing on diet, exercise, rest, and overall mental health. I became intentional about learning to listen and trust myself. Meditation and mindfulness were a huge part of my healing process.

We change when the pain of where we are becomes greater than the fear of what comes next. All of the obstacles I faced showed me that though change is scary, it doesn't have to be painful. You get to decide how you enter new experiences because anxiety and excitement are two sides of the same coin, both born from uncertainty, but your mindset determines how you approach the unknown. The best thing you can do is flow with change because it is the one certainty in life.

Surround yourself with people who empower you with accountability. Never stop making yourself the priority or let your dreams take a back seat. Know that the right partner will make room in the front seat for both of your dreams. Hold yourself accountable, always giving yourself grace and space to grow.

ACHIEVING SUCCESS

I see success through the lives changed by sharing my story and guiding others through my book and coaching program. I have used every obstacle as a springboard to the next phase of my career and accomplished things I never thought I would by starting businesses and achieving my childhood dream of writing a book. Most importantly, I learned to measure my success by the lives I touch, not by the money I make or outward accolades.

I plan to continue coaching women helping them uncover their uniqueness and leverage those strengths to achieve the life of their dreams. I will continue teaching the importance of wellness and balance, permitting women to define success for themselves.

REFLECTION AND ACTION

I challenge others to re-introduce yourself to YOU. Become intimately familiar with your gifts and begin using them more intentionally and fruitfully. Compare your life with the vision you dare to dream, and then make concrete goals to be accountable to yourself to make that vision your reality.

www.darlenetaylor.com
www.darlenetaylor.com/social-links
darlene@darlenetaylor.com

LIFESTYLE &
Wellness

by Alina Timofeeva

FROM CLEANING TOILETS TO GLOBAL STAGES: THE EDUCATIONAL JOURNEY OF ALINA TIMOFEEVA

Alina Timofeeva's journey is a powerful testament to resilience and the transformative power of education. Born in a small village in post-Soviet Russia, her path from washing toilets at McDonald's in Russia to becoming a prominent figure in technology in London, UK, underscores her unwavering determination and passion for learning. This article explores Alina's educational journey, highlighting how her relentless pursuit of knowledge paved the way for her success.

EARLY BEGINNINGS AND SELF-EDUCATION

Growing up in a poor family, Alina was raised with the expectation that her future would be confined to traditional gender roles. However, she felt destined for more. Alina's thirst for knowledge became evident early on. At just eight years old, she taught herself English using old audiotapes—a skill that would become invaluable. Her academic potential was recognised when she won the prestigious Moscow State University Olympiad at 14, granting her direct admission to a specialised mathematics school. This achievement marked the beginning of a series of academic successes.

Continuing her trajectory of excellence, Alina secured another Olympiad win at 16, earning a full scholarship to Moscow State University (MSU). At MSU, she pursued both a Bachelor's and a Master's degree in Mathematics, honing her analytical and problem-solving skills in a rigorous academic environment.

EXPANDING HORIZONS AT THE LONDON SCHOOL OF ECONOMICS

Alina's academic journey extended beyond Russia. Determined to broaden her horizons, she pursued a second Master's degree in Risk and Finance at the prestigious London School of Economics (LSE). This transition came with its challenges, as she navigated the competitive UK job market, often feeling out of place among peers from more privileged backgrounds. Nevertheless, her solid academic foundation and determination saw her through these obstacles.

OVERCOMING BARRIERS

Despite her impressive educational background, Alina faced significant challenges in her early career. Navigating societal expectations and professional etiquette in the UK proved challenging. Her tenacity was tested as she applied for 500 jobs and faced 497 rejections before securing a graduate analyst position at Accenture. This experience highlighted her resilience—a hallmark of her journey.

Alina faced further challenges in her career, particularly during her first promotion attempt. With the guidance of a senior mentor, she rediscovered her confidence and self-worth, leading to a successful promotion just a year after being deemed as failing. Her perseverance paid off, as she was promoted four times in four years—an impressive feat in the male-dominated tech industry.

TENACITY SHAPING CAREER JOURNEY

Today, in her early thirties, Alina is a multi-award-winning strategic advisor in Data & Technology, serving the C-suite of major financial services organizations. She holds a board position at The Chartered Institute for IT and is a thought leader, sought-after speaker, and role model in the tech industry. Her work with leading consulting firms like Oliver Wyman, KPMG, and Accenture has earned her numerous accolades, including Digital Leader of the Year, Digital Transformation Leader, Cloud Professional of the Year, and Most Inspirational Individual of the Year.

SPEAKING ON GLOBAL STAGES

Alina has become a prominent voice on Data and Technology, speaking at high-profile events like the World Economic Forum, London Tech Week, and Money 20/20. She has also shared her insights at prestigious institutions, including the University of Oxford and the London School of Economics. Her TEDx talk, "Fail but Never Give Up," has garnered over 510,000 views, translated into 23 languages, and ranks among the top 10 most-watched TEDx talks released in December 2021. In it, she illustrates how failing an exam for a fast-food chain can lead to three university degrees, career success, and becoming a role model for women in technology.

LIFELONG LEARNING AND MENTORSHIP

Throughout her career, Alina has emphasized the importance of lifelong learning and mentorship. Her journey has taught her the significance of acquiring not just knowledge but also the ability to navigate unspoken societal codes. By seeking mentorship and continually learning, she has overcome biases and thrived in traditionally male-dominated fields.

GIVING BACK

Alina's commitment to education extends beyond her achievements. She founded Unique. Bold. You, an initiative supporting individuals from diverse backgrounds to persevere despite failures. She actively coaches others, particularly women in technology and those from underprivileged backgrounds, guiding them through their educational and professional journeys. As a TEDx speaker and LinkedIn Top Voice in Technology, she aims to inspire 50 million people globally to view failure as an opportunity for growth, whether in technology or personal endeavours.

Alina Timofeeva's educational journey serves as a powerful reminder of the transformative potential of education. From teaching herself English to excelling at two of the world's most prestigious universities, her story is one of relentless pursuit of knowledge. Alina's journey demonstrates that with determination, resilience, and a commitment to learning, one can overcome even the most daunting challenges.

GET IN TOUCH: www.linkedin.com/in/atimofeeva

Breaking Barriers: Transforming Adversity into Leadership as an Immigrant Woman

by Tamanna Ramesh

A decade ago, a determined young woman from a small town in India arrived in the United States, fueled by dreams of a better future. Despite the promise of new opportunities, her journey was fraught with challenges—cultural adjustments, language barriers, workplace toxicity, and the complexities of the U.S. immigration system. Yet, her unwavering commitment to personal and professional growth powered her through these obstacles.

From the outset, integrating into the American workplace proved difficult due to cultural differences and the complex immigration system. The Green Card process was particularly daunting, with the EB2 category's wait time exceeding 130 years—a formidable barrier. Professionally, she faced pay equity issues and the constant need to prove herself, especially as a woman in STEM. These obstacles were compounded by harassment, discrimination, and the everyday stress of navigating a new country. Nevertheless, she transformed these adversities into opportunities for growth.

Her journey was marked by an impressive achievement: securing $135,000 in scholarships and assistantships, which funded her STEM graduate degree and part-time MBA program in the U.S. This financial support was crucial, allowing her to focus on her education without incurring significant debt. Over the years, she honed her networking strategies and perfected her negotiation tactics, landing dream jobs at Fortune 500 companies and making five unconventional career pivots. Each move was a calculated step towards building her personal brand and significantly increasing her compensation.

A defining moment in her life came when she secured her Green Card at the age of 29, breaking through the historic wait time barrier by qualifying under the EB1 category—one of the most challenging categories for Indian nationals. This achievement was not just a personal victory but a profound symbol of new beginnings. Free from immigration uncertainty, she could finally pursue her aspirations fully.

With renewed determination, she committed to continuous personal and professional development, advancing from a researcher to a director at a Fortune 100 company. This remarkable progression was driven by hard work, perseverance, and the invaluable support of mentors and sponsors who nurtured her potential. She also took on leadership roles in professional organizations, notably with the Institute of Food Technologists, where she served as Chair of the Product Development Division and the Women's Resource Group. These roles amplified her influence and established her as a thought leader in the food and beverage industry.

Throughout her journey, she faced numerous unseen challenges: overperforming while underpaid, dealing with bad managers, experiencing burnout and imposter syndrome, and confronting biases and systemic barriers. While the highs on her LinkedIn profile are visible, the lows—marked by harassment, bullying, and the grueling immigration process—were equally significant. Despite these struggles, she chose to fight, paving her own path with resilience and determination.

Her experiences taught her that success is not solely defined by titles or financial gain but by the freedom and empowerment to pursue one's own path. Perseverance, adaptability, and continuous learning were essential to overcoming adversity and achieving success.

To those navigating similar challenges, she advises remaining resilient and proactive. Seek out mentors and sponsors for guidance and support, and invest in continuous learning to enhance your skills and adaptability. Challenges often present opportunities for significant personal growth and success.

Today, she stands as a leader at a Fortune 100 company and the founder of Spark Career Services, dedicated to supporting underrepresented individuals in their career journeys. Through Spark Career Services, she helps others overcome barriers, achieve career advancement, and drive equity in the workplace. Her goal is to empower one million individuals to break through barriers and achieve career fulfillment, with a commitment to fostering workplace wellness and championing purpose-driven careers.

Call to Action for All the Amazing Women Out There:

- **ASK** for those high-visibility projects, raises, and promotions that you deserve.
- **BALANCE** by prioritizing your well-being to avoid burnout and undue stress.
- **CHALLENGE** biases and systemic barriers that stand in your way.

feeding the minds that feed the world

Contact:
www.sparkcareerservices.com
www.linkedin.com/company/spark-career-services
www.linkedin.com/in/tamannaramesh
www.instagram.com/spark_your_career

sparkcareerservicesllc@gmail.com

The SHE RISES STUDIOS PODCAST

The She Rises Studios podcast is dedicated to empowering women like you to reach their full potential and live their best lives. With inspiring stories, insightful interviews, and practical advice from experts in different industries, our podcast is your go-to source for information, inspiration, and motivation. Join us as we explore topics like:

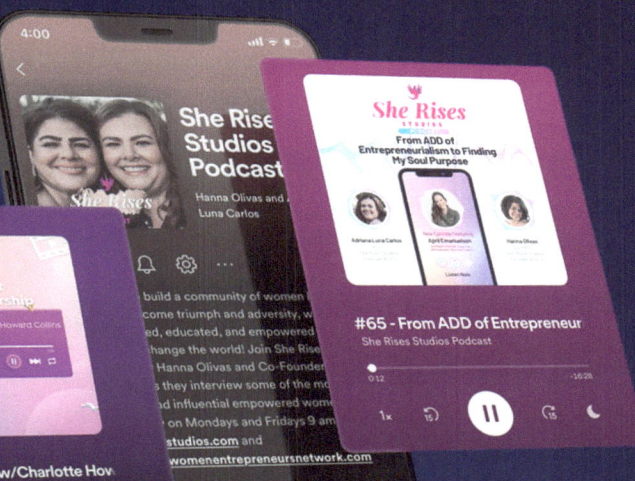

- Overcoming self-doubt and limiting beliefs
- Building and running a successful business
- Building confidence and Self-esteem
- Navigating career transitions
- Starting and growing a business
- Balancing work and family life
- Improving physical and mental health
- Finding meaning and purpose in life
- So many more

Our guests include successful entrepreneurs, inspiring thought leaders, and everyday women who have overcome challenges and achieved their dreams. Each episode is packed with actionable tips and strategies to help you take your life to the next level.

by Angelica Kapsis

PIONEERING VETERAN TRANSFORMING U.S. ELECTIONS

Angelica Kapsis, President of VotRite

Angelica Kapsis is the President and Co-Founder of VotRite, a South Florida company dedicated to re-shaping how elections are conducted in the United States. With Angelica at the helm, VotRite is determined to make the future of local, state, and national elections more accessible, more secure, and more transparent for all. VotRite is also committed to maintaining an environment free from bullying and harassment. Angelica ensures her team is treated with dignity while being held to above higher than average standards for their performance.

Angelica is a dedicated professional with a diverse background in forensic science, psychology, and human services. She holds a Masters in Science in Forensic Science from National University as well as a Bachelor of Science in Psychology from Stony Brook University, showcasing her strong commitment to education and continuous learning.

In addition to her incredible academic career, Angelica is an accomplished Navy Veteran. She has built her life and career on fighting for those in need. As the President and Co-Founder of VotRite, Angelica has been instrumental in developing strategies to enhance voting software accessibility, particularly focusing on ADA (Americans with Disabilities Act) compliance and preferences for individuals with disabilities.

Angelica is also the Founder at Scorpion Fitness Centers, a position that reflects her passion for promoting health and wellness. She has crafted unique fitness plans for members and leads classes, including those catered to individuals with disabilities, in order to guarantee success for clients.

Beyond her professional endeavors, Angelica's dedication to community service is evident through her involvement in various volunteer activities. Angelica has worked as a firefighter, a mentor, and has advocated for at-risk populations. She is also a NASM Certified Personal Trainer and holds CPR & First Aid Certification. Angelica's multifaceted skill set, coupled with her unwavering dedication to social causes, positions her as a versatile and compassionate professional dedicated to making a truly positive impact in her community and beyond.

Angelica is a passionate advocate for technological innovation and creativity. Her company, VotRite, stands at the forefront of electoral innovation, offering cutting-edge voting solutions designed to revolutionize the democratic process. Committed to inclusivity and integrity, VotRite ensures that every voter, regardless of ability or background, can participate in hack-proof elections with confidence. With a steadfast dedication to neutrality and transparency, VotRite's unbiased approach guarantees that election results are trustworthy and immune to contestation. By prioritizing ADA compliance, customizable features, and a commitment to impartiality, VotRite is leading the charge towards fair and equitable elections, where every voice is heard and every vote counts.

To work beside her in achieving her mission, Angelica has selected only those that share her passionate dream and have the knowledge to follow through. Jim Kapsis, VotRite's CEO, has extensive management and technology capabilities and has been the leader of various voting companies in the last 30 years. He has created two patents for voting integration and copyright software. Christopher H. Baum, the company's Chief Compliance Officer, has spent more than 30 years delivering high-quality IT analysis and services on the use of technology in government and in the election industry in particular. Baum currently manages certification processes and ensures election integrity.

As of 2024, VotRite has been officially nominated for this year's Technology Innovator Awards hosted by Innovation in Business, as well as nominated for the 2024 Education and Training Awards hosted by Corporate Vision. It is because of Angelica's unwavering dedication and determination that her company has achieved success, and she has persevered in spite of pushback from other Electronic Voting Machine organizations. Angelica has offered her knowledge and expertise to a variety of media outlets, including the podcast Everyday's Saturday - USMC Veteran and Authority Magazine. She will also be featured in upcoming episodes of the HomeFront Sitrep Podcast as well as the Implementors Podcast.

RISING FROM THE ASHES: CANDYK'S JOURNEY OF RESILIENCE AND LEADERSHIP

C *andyK's* story is a testament to resilience and the indomitable human spirit. Overcoming medical complications and homelessness, she transformed her suffering into advocacy and leadership. Her journey was deeply influenced by her parents, both dedicated advocates.

Her father, a Vietnam War veteran, often recounted his experiences, sharing the profound impact of the war on his health and life. Despite his challenges, he was active in the VFW, NAACP, and the Urban League, while her mother also contributed to the NAACP, Urban League, and Church. They instilled in CandyK the importance of standing up for what is right and working towards legislative change.

Growing up, CandyK was inspired by her father's resilience and dedication. Despite his strictness, he encouraged her to work hard and uphold her beliefs. Witnessing his struggle with illnesses caused by Agent Orange, including cancer, motivated CandyK to honor his sacrifices. In high school, she balanced rigorous academic courses while participating in sports like track, cheerleading, and gymnastics, all while helping her father heal. She also started working at the VA at age 12, participating in work summer school and cultural programs, and attending a Catholic preschool and an all-white elementary school as the only African American child in her class.

CandyK's upbringing in a diverse environment taught her to embrace her authentic self and fostered respect from her classmates. Even in the face of racism from some classmates' parents during the 1970s, she and her friends stood firm, ignoring outdated prejudices.

Her pivotal moment came during a harrowing recovery. After multiple surgeries to remove all her female organs and right lymph node due to complications from a birth control medical device, she nearly lost her life and everything she owned. The trauma resulted in chronic homelessness, exacerbated by excessive hospitalizations. CandyK was devastated and desperate for answers. How could a birth control device, deemed safe and used by millions, lead to such catastrophic consequences?

Her ordeal extended beyond the physical consequences. Homelessness exposed her to inhumane treatment, as numerous women's organizations, government agencies, and even Planned Parenthood ignored her pleas for help. This indifference deeply affected CandyK and her two sons, amplifying the trauma of losing everything she had worked for, including her home and irreplaceable family heirlooms.

Financial distress further compounded her suffering. Abandoned by her ex-fiancé, CandyK relied on short-term support from her mother and limited financial assistance from her father, a Vietnam Veteran on a fixed income. Hospitalizations continued due to post-surgery complications, highlighting the profound impact of medical device trauma.

During her journey, CandyK met many homeless women living in appalling conditions, fighting for survival with no support. She vowed to advocate for them once she regained her strength. The risks homeless women faced—rape, hunger, trafficking, and drugs—were incomprehensible to many, including organizations that claimed to help women. Despite repeated rejections from the Social Security Administration and other entities, CandyK's resolve to not give up on herself only strengthened.

With no response from multiple law firms, CandyK took matters into her own hands. While healing, she began researching the top ten pharmaceutical corporations in the United States, tracing their histories back to the 1600s. She uncovered how internationally owned pharmaceutical companies started marketing birth control pills in the U.S. to dominate the industry, leading to many unreported adverse impacts on women.

Her disturbing findings fueled her determination to advocate for women's reproductive health. CandyK pledged to ensure that no woman or child would ever endure the medical trauma or homelessness she experienced. Her mission became clear: to advocate for women and safeguard them from such devastating ordeals.

CandyK became a voice for the voiceless, securing roles as a public speaker during the 2016 Presidential Campaign, briefly having her own show with WCOBM in Hollywood, CA, and becoming a Federally Registered Contractor based on her pharmaceutical research submitted to Obama. She became a member of the U.S. Women's Chamber of Commerce, participated in the National Small Business Association boards in Washington, D.C., and attended the Leadership Institute of Virginia. She became a certified Homeless Women's Advocate with the City of Los Angeles and a Certified Humanitarian Consultant with the U.S. Institute of Diplomacy and Human Rights.

Despite facing severe backlash, including threats, blacklisting, and financial ruin, CandyK's resolve never wavered. Instead, she focused on her spiritual healing to build her own businesses to continue providing vital services to those in need. CandyK's life and career embody strength, courage, and resilience, shaped by her parents' advocacy and service. She stands as a beacon of hope, continually fighting for justice and equality in America.

In memory of her grandmother Martha Williamson, her sister Jillion Camper who passed in May 2023, and her Chihuahua Teaspoon of 15 years who passed in May 2024.

CONNECT WITH HER

- www.candyksboutiquefashionz.com
- www.humanitariansnetwork.com
- www.patreon.com/TransformHTHN
- www.linkedin.com/in/cabiri
- www.consumer2savlives.wordpress.com
- www.youtube.com/@chozen1snetworkclubroyalhi329
- www.facebook.com/kaila.truths

by Kay Harper

FROM FARM ROOTS TO COUNTRY MUSIC'S RISING STAR

I grew up in a small farming town in southern Michigan, a place where hard work was the way of life. My grandfather was a third-generation dairy farmer, and my parents ran a vegetable farm, teaching me the value of perseverance and dedication from a young age. My early life was filled with the sounds of country music legends like Patsy Cline and Loretta Lynn, which sparked my passion for music. I sang in school choirs, taught myself guitar through online tutorials, and dreamed of a future where my voice could be heard by the world.

However, life wasn't always kind. My childhood was marked by the absence of my biological father and the presence of an abusive and manipulative step-dad. Feeling the sting of abandonment and dealing with the traumas of a turbulent homelife left deep scars. The emotional turmoil led to significant self-esteem and anger issues that plagued me for years.

The challenges continued to mount during my senior year of high school when I lost a friend to suicide. This was a devastating blow, especially since I was also struggling with my own mental health and had been considering suicide as well. Shortly after, I found myself pregnant at 18, trapped in a toxic relationship and repeating the same cycles from my childhood. By 25, I was divorced and trying to navigate life as a single mother, all while dealing with the fallout of my unresolved traumas and a near diagnosis of borderline personality disorder.

Also, the compilation of no's from singing contests and the reality TV industry (The Voice, AGT, and American Idol) continued to wear on me as well. Although I had been close multiple times even gaining private interviews with producers, I ultimately always received a no. I was in this headspace where I thought the only way to make it was to be noticed by these people and each no was a letdown.

The turning point in my journey came when I hit the age of 30. Realizing that life was passing me by, I knew I had to take control of my destiny. It was a moment of self-reckoning where I decided that enough was enough. I could no longer wait for a miracle or validation from the outside world.

I began to actively pursue my passion for music, starting with local gigs and open mic nights. This was a huge step for someone who had always struggled with anxiety and body image issues. I also sought therapy during my divorce and after to address my mental health challenges, which helped me develop coping mechanisms and a healthier mindset. Reconnecting with my biological father & biological family provided some closure and helped me understand and forgive the past.

In addition to my musical pursuits, I leveraged my professional skills in marketing and PR to build my brand. I taught myself how to handle everything from photoshoots to social media management, ensuring that I had complete control over my career. The culmination of these efforts was recording my debut single, "Freight Train," in Nashville with the help of some incredibly talented musicians.

One of the most important lessons I learned is the power of resilience. Despite the setbacks and challenges, each "no" I received from reality TV shows like American Idol and The Voice only fueled my determination. I also learned the importance of self-belief and taking proactive steps toward my goals. Waiting for someone else to recognize your worth is a path to nowhere; you have to be your own biggest advocate.

For those facing similar challenges, my advice is to never give up on your dreams. Take actionable steps, no matter how small, toward your goals. Seek out support systems, whether it's therapy, friends, or family, and don't be afraid to ask for help. Remember that setbacks are just setups

Kay Harper, hailing from the small farming towns of Waterloo & Napoleon in southern Michigan, combines her rich roots with a diverse musical palette. Growing up surrounded by the sounds of classic country legends like Patsy Cline and Loretta Lynn, Kay's passion for music blossomed early on. Now, she's bringing her heartfelt storytelling and soulful voice to the world with the release of her debut single "Freight Train." This track showcases Kay's journey, resilience, and the raw emotion that defines her unique sound. Don't miss out on this rising star's powerful debut, available on all streaming platforms.

for comebacks. Use your experiences, no matter how painful, as fuel to propel you forward.

Today, I am proud to say that I am thriving both personally and professionally. "Freight Train" has been well-received, and I continue to perform and connect with audiences who find solace and inspiration in my music. Overcoming adversity has not only contributed to my success but also shaped me into a stronger, more compassionate individual.

Looking ahead, I aim to continue making music that resonates with people and tells authentic stories of struggle and triumph. I want to use my platform to advocate for mental health awareness and support others who are dealing with similar challenges. My goal is to inspire others to believe in themselves and pursue their dreams, no matter the obstacles.

I encourage you, the reader, to reflect on your own challenges and consider how you can turn them into opportunities for growth. Take that first step toward overcoming your obstacles and remember that you are not alone. By sharing our stories and supporting one another, we can create a world where resilience and perseverance lead to incredible achievements.

www.kayharperofficial.com
www.facebook.com/kayharperofficial
www.instagram.com/kayharperofficial
www.tiktok.com/kayharperofficial
www.distrokid.com/hyperfollow/kayharper/freight-train

JOIN OUR COMMUNITY

We believe the future is female and that we are better and stronger together. This group is NOT just for entrepreneurs but for women in general of all ages and from all walks of life.

www.bit.ly/srscommunitygroup

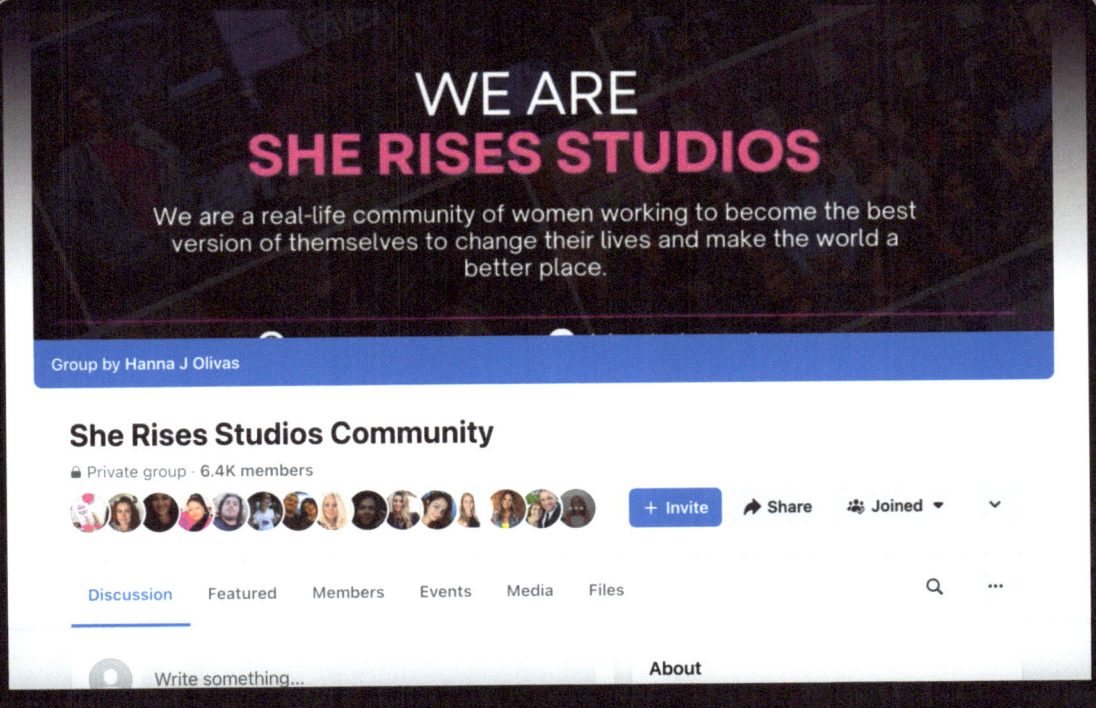